English Class 3

Young World 1

Activity Book

Illya Arnet-Clark
Corinne Lanz

Klett und Balmer Verlag Zug

Our classroom

Classroom and colours

1 Find, count and write the numbers. Read the text out.

3	desks		pencils		blackboards		chairs		schoolbags
	doors		books		pencil cases		rubbers		ruler
	boys and girls								

2 Colour:

desks = green
pencils = blue
blackboards = black
chairs = brown
schoolbags = red
books = yellow
doors = grey
rubbers = pink
pencil cases = orange
ruler = black and white
boys and girls = all colours

3 Match the numbers.

1	three	eleven	7
2	five	seven	8
3	six	twelve	9
4	two	ten	10
5	one	eight	11
6	four	nine	12

4 *Listen and colour.*

5 *Complete and read the numbers out.*

6 *Colour snake 1 and read the colours to your partner. Listen to your partner and colour snake 2.*

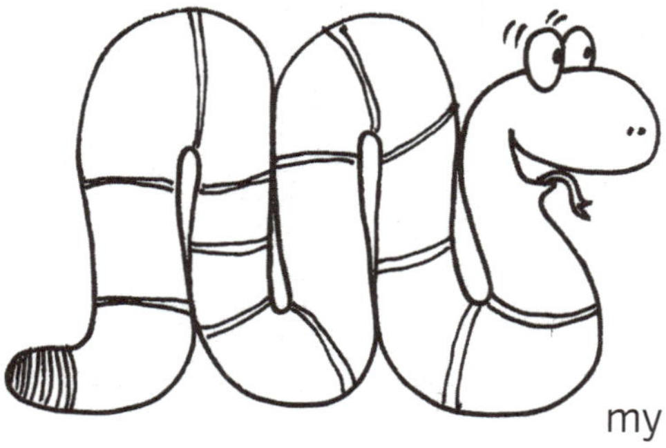

my snake 1

your snake 2

You and me

This is me and my family

1 Stick in a family photo or draw your family.

2 Write down.

Hello. My name is .

I am from . I live in .

I speak .

This is me and my family.

Switzerland

3 Number the cities on the map.
1 Zurich
2 Lugano
3 Lucerne
4 Geneva
5 Berne

4 Where do you live?
Make a cross.

5 Fill in the boxes:
north, south, east, west

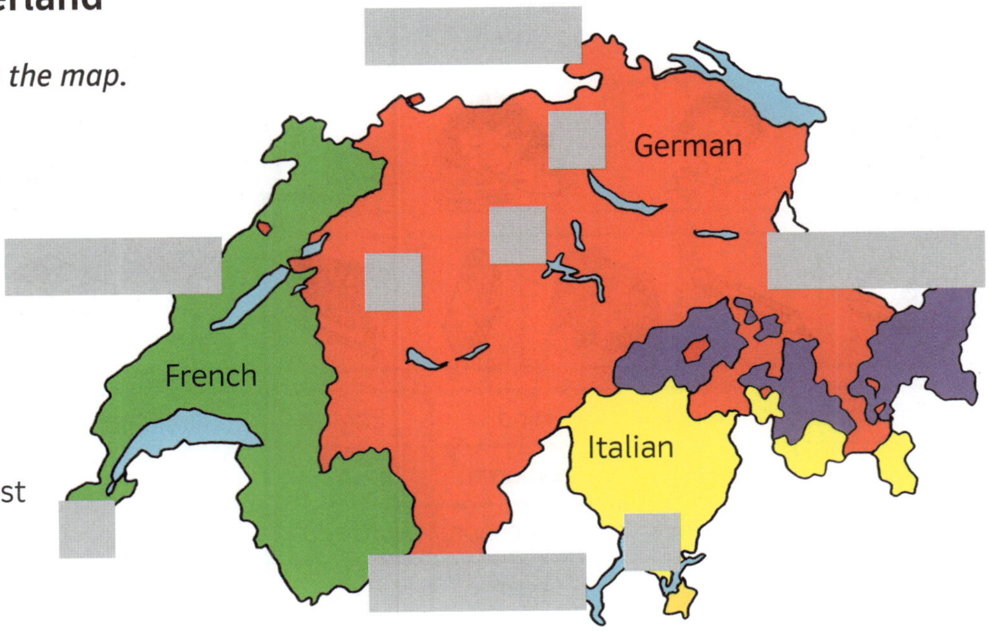

6 *Listen and tick.*

Mike lives in	☐ New York	☐ New Delhi	☐ London
	☐ Johannesburg	☐ Vancouver	☐ Perth
Mike speaks	☐ English	☐ French	☐ Italian
	☐ Hindi	☐ Xhosa	☐ German

Shanoo lives in	☐ New York	☐ New Delhi	☐ London
	☐ Johannesburg	☐ Vancouver	☐ Perth
She speaks	☐ English	☐ French	☐ Italian
	☐ Hindi	☐ Xhosa	☐ German

Julie lives in	☐ New York	☐ New Delhi	☐ London
	☐ Johannesburg	☐ Vancouver	☐ Perth
She speaks	☐ English	☐ French	☐ Italian
	☐ Hindi	☐ Xhosa	☐ German

Afzal lives in	☐ New York	☐ New Delhi	☐ London
	☐ Johannesburg	☐ Vancouver	☐ Perth
He speaks	☐ English	☐ French	☐ Italian
	☐ Hindi	☐ Xhosa	☐ German

David lives in	☐ New York	☐ New Delhi	☐ London
	☐ Johannesburg	☐ Vancouver	☐ Perth
He speaks	☐ English	☐ French	☐ Italian
	☐ Hindi	☐ Xhosa	☐ German

Sue lives in	☐ New York	☐ New Delhi	☐ London
	☐ Johannesburg	☐ Vancouver	☐ Perth
She speaks	☐ English	☐ French	☐ Italian
	☐ Hindi	☐ Xhosa	☐ German

7 *Find the odd one out.*

French	Italian	Hindi	English	language	German	Xhosa
mum	dad	grandma	mummy	father	daddy	mother
New Delhi	New York	Johannesburg	Switzerland	Berne	Vancouver	London
north	south	east	west	northeast	southwest	city

Me and my family

8 Complete the form.

My name is ...
I am from ...
I live in ...
This is my family.
This ... my mother.
Name: ...
This ... my ...
Name: ...
This ... ...
And t... ... ...
Name: ...

Marco's family

9 Who is missing?
Complete the gaps with the correct words.

10 Look at your family and find out.

My sisters and brothers:

My mother

My mother's sisters and brothers:

My father

My father's sisters and brothers:

My grandmother

My grandmother's sisters and brothers:

My grandfather

My grandfather's sisters and brothers:

My grandmother

My grandmother's sisters and brothers:

My grandfather

My grandfather's sisters and brothers:

My mother's sister is my aunt.

My mother's brother is my uncle.

My father's sister is

My father's brother is

Riddle
Your mother and father have a child.
It isn't your brother. It isn't your sister.
Who is it?

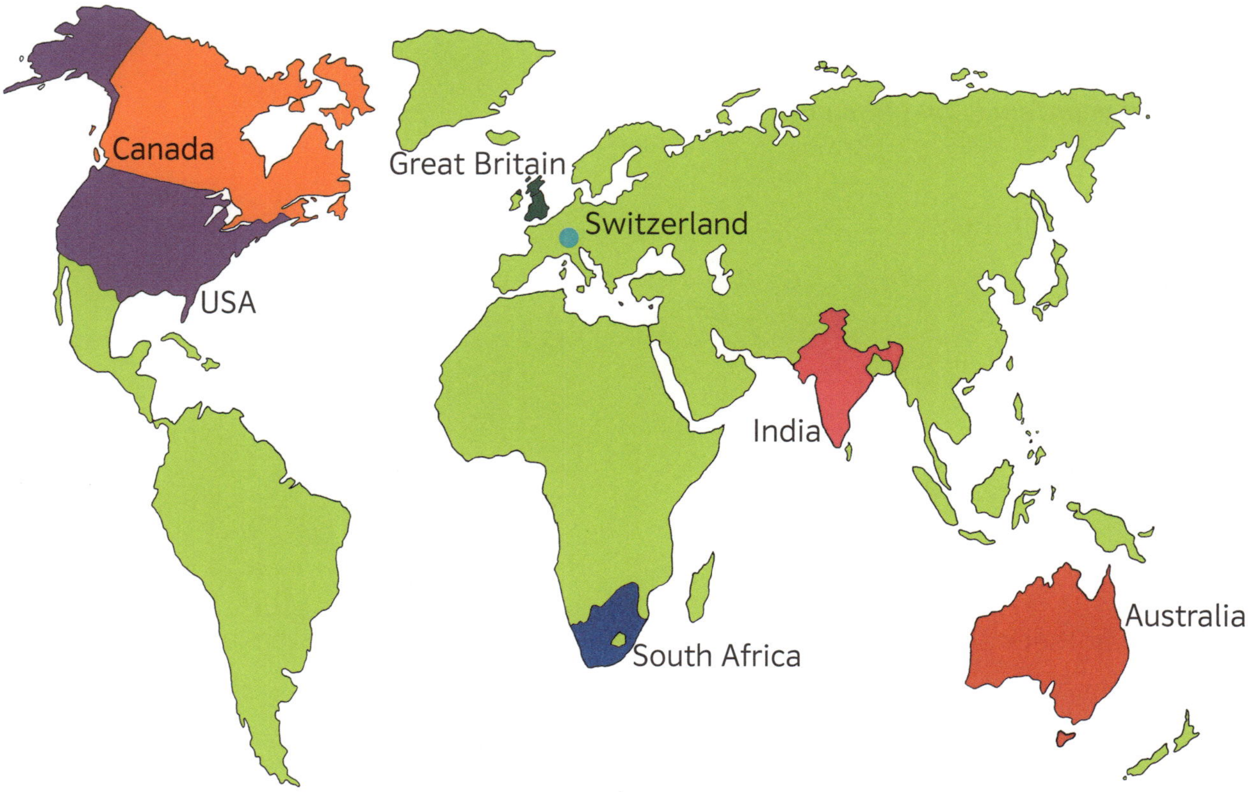

11 *Do you know these flags? Write the names of the countries (look at the map).*

German

Italian

French

Hindi

English

Xhosa

12 *Draw a line from the languages to the flags.*

Puzzles

13 Word maze
Find and colour the hidden words.

dog	family
cat	mother
pencil	father
sister	east
brother	name
grandpa	north
grandma	

b	h	s	w	q	x	k	n	c	v	e	t	b	b
i	p	l	b	v	c	a	g	m	n	x	e	k	h
k	k	m	c	x	p	k	m	r	q	e	a	o	m
t	z	r	s	d	x	y	l	k	a	a	s	m	b
m	t	r	n	n	c	a	t	w	v	n	t	f	d
a	p	a	z	x	m	d	o	g	b	t	d	o	k
c	r	y	r	f	a	m	i	l	y	m	r	m	o
g	x	f	c	n	m	s	k	f	h	n	m	g	a
b	v	a	x	d	a	i	r	h	g	o	o	p	w
c	z	t	g	k	m	s	e	q	s	r	t	x	d
p	u	h	b	r	o	t	h	e	r	t	h	p	o
m	e	e	a	z	c	e	m	w	q	h	e	e	r
d	w	r	m	y	v	r	e	t	o	b	r	m	x
j	k	n	a	m	e	p	e	n	c	i	l	k	g
r	d	h	a	q	y	g	j	w	e	m	b	d	h

14 Crossword
Fill the gaps.

15 Evaluation

I like page ____ in the Pupil's Book and page ____ in the Activity Book.

The funniest word: ____. I can say: ____

I remember these words: ____

This unit was: ☐ great ☺ ☐ ok 😐 ☐ boring ☹ ☐ hard 💣

My body

This is Mr Line Man

1 Unscramble the words and match.

mar

oets

ahde

gle

eetf

sinferg

danh

ofot

2 Draw Mr Line Man for the actions and complete the sentences.

1

2

3

4

5

6

1 My Mr Line Man can run.

2 Mr Line Man can jump up.

3 can stand on one foot.

4 kick a ball.

5

6

Project

3 Make a Mr Line Man.

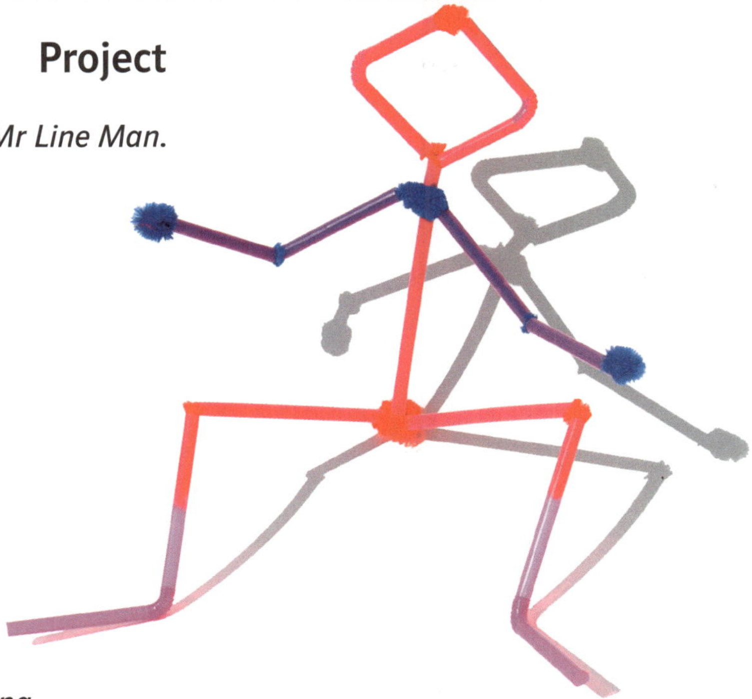

4 Sing a song.

Head and shoulders, knees and toes, knees and toes,
Eyes and ears and mouth and nose,
Head and shoulders, knees and toes, knees and toes.

"Thumbs up"

5 Do the chant. Fill in the gaps.

I kick with my ________

and run with my ________

I catch and throw with my ________ and hands.

I touch with my ________ and point them at you.

And thumbs up means it's okay.

I look with my ________

Yes, I see you!

And with my ________ I smile at you.

I hear with my ________ and smell with my nose.

And thumbs up means it's okay.

My face

6 Draw your face.

my eyes

brown eyes
blue eyes
green eyes
black eyes
grey eyes
yellow eyes
red eyes

my nose

long nose
short nose
up nose
down nose

my hair

straight hair
curly hair
long hair
short hair

brown hair
blonde hair
red hair
black hair
orange hair
blue hair

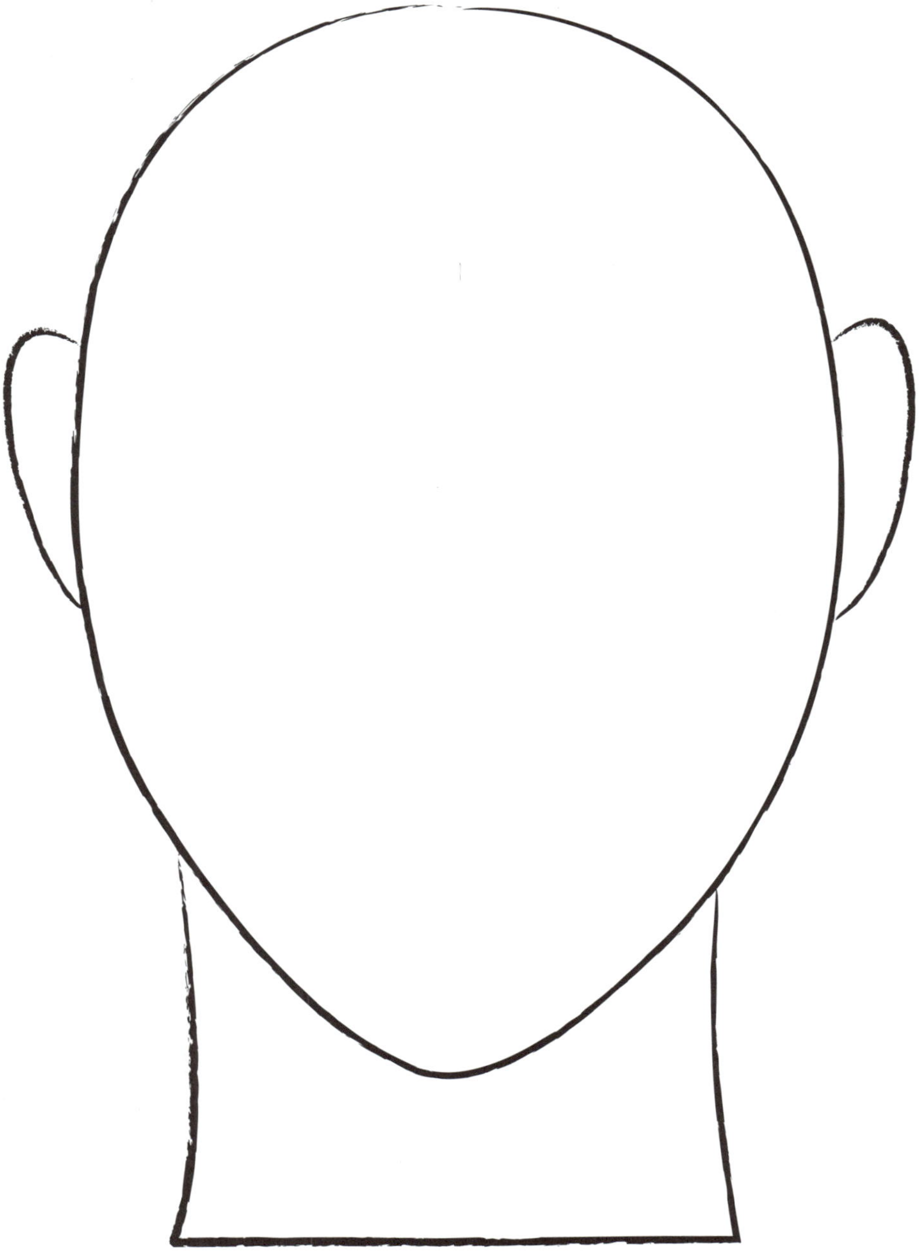

7 Describe your face.

I have eyes.

I have a nose

and hair.

I don't have yellow eyes!

I don't have

Questionnaire

8 Ask your friends and fill in ✔ yes or ✘ no.

Do you have a long nose?
Yes, I do.
Do you have brown eyes?
No, I don't.

	A Name:	B Name:
a long nose		
a short nose		
brown eyes		
blue eyes		
green eyes		
grey eyes		
long hair		
short hair		
curly hair		
brown hair		
blonde hair		
black hair		
red hair		

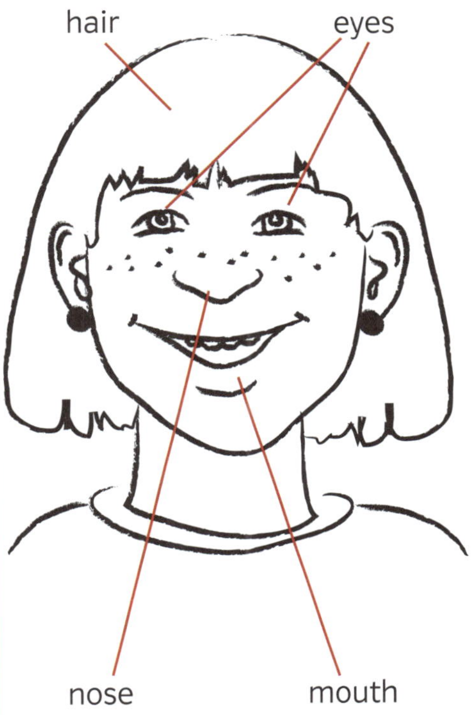

9 Play a game.
Who am I?
I have green eyes and a short nose.
I have long, brown hair.
Who am I?

10 Now, let's do the hokey pokey!

My size

11 How tall are you?
Measure and fill in.

	Date 1	Date 2
body		
arm		
leg		
head		
nose		
ear		
hand		
thumb		
big toe		
neck		

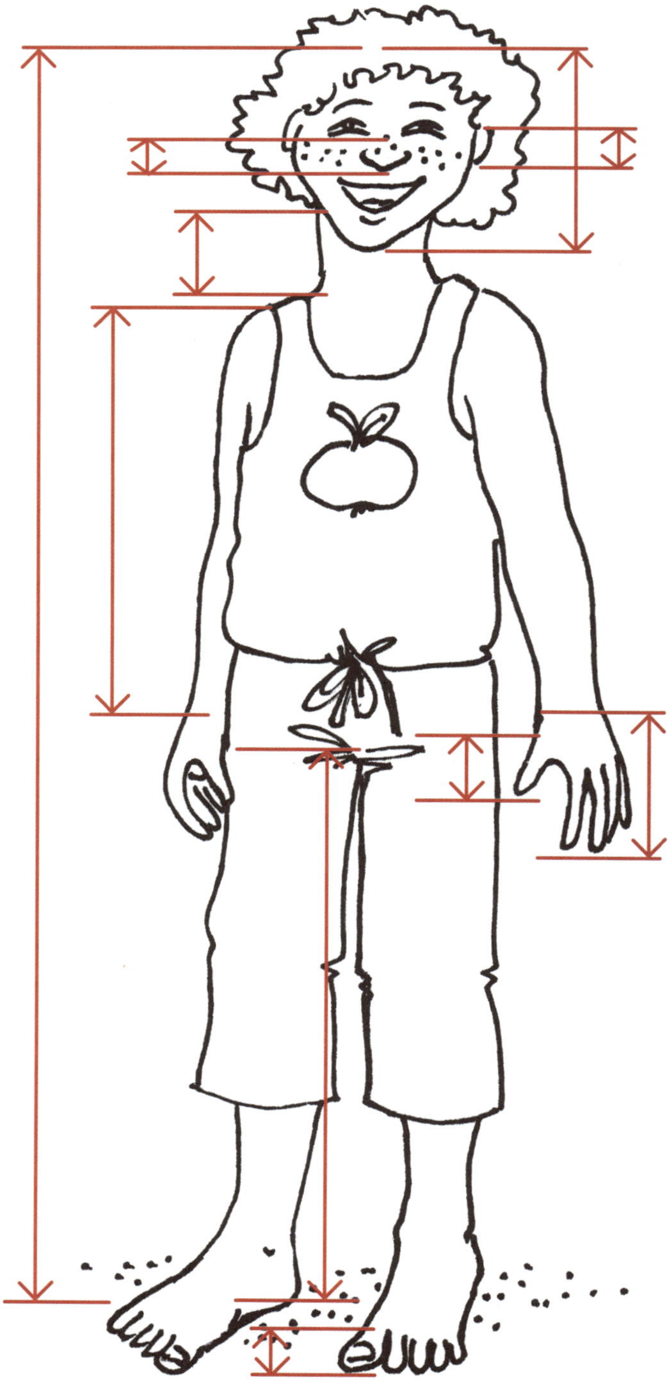

12 Describe your body.

I am ________ cm tall.
My arm is ________ cm long.
My leg is ________ cm long.
etc.

In a year you grow about 3– 8 cm.
You can measure your height every year
(i.e. on your birthday) to see how much you grow.

Inside the body

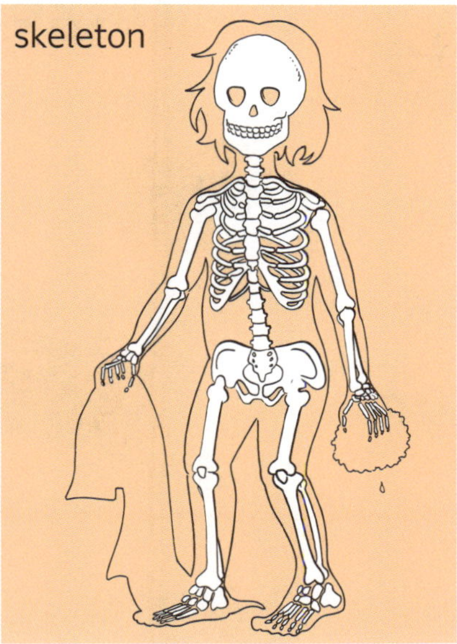

The skeleton is made of bones.
The bones protect your brain, heart and lungs.

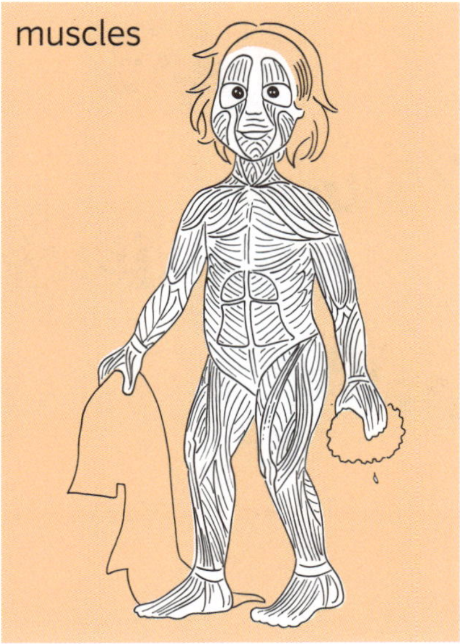

The muscles connect the bones.
The muscles help you jump, bend and run.

13 Feel your bones and find out.
How many bones?

There are ______ bones in my finger.

There are ______ bones in my thumb.

There are ______ bones in my hand.

14 Listen and do.

15 Quiz. Listen and tick.

1 Your smallest bones are in your	☐ ear 	☐ fingers 	☐ toes 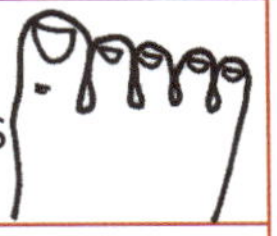
2 Your headbone is called 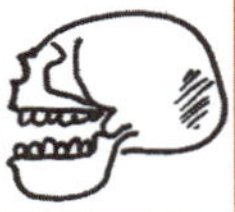	☐ rib	☐ heart	☐ skull
3 You have	☐ 46 bones	☐ 1006 bones	☐ 206 bones
4 To smile, you need 	☐ 26 muscles	☐ 24 muscles	☐ 92 muscles
5 Your biggest muscle is in your	☐ leg 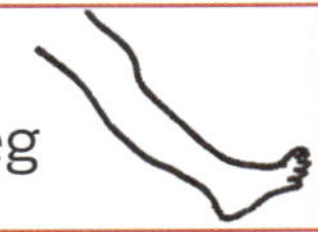	☐ bottom 	☐ arm 

16 Draw a picture with the words.

hand leg finger foot mouth neck arm nose hair eye shoulder head

17 Evaluation

I like page ___ in the Pupil's Book and page ___ in the Activity Book.

The funniest word: ___. I can say: ___

I remember these words: ___

This unit was: ☐ great ☺ ☐ ok 😐 ☐ boring ☹ ☐ hard 💣

Apples and crisps

What do you like?

1 Listen and tick yes or no.

	Sue		Afzal		And you? What do you like?	
	yes	no	yes	no	yes	no
bananas						
apples						
oranges						
carrots						
crisps						
sandwiches						

Her favourite food:

His favourite food:

My favourite food:

2 Ask three friends and complete the chart. Write yes or no.

Do you like …?

Name	bananas	tomatoes	fish fingers	hamburgers

3 You are back from the supermarket. What have you got? Write the words.

4 Look at the things in this list. What makes you run faster and longer, what makes you feel good and healthy, and what makes you feel tired and full?

	ENERGY  run faster and longer	VITAMINS  feel good and healthy	 feel tired and full
one sandwich			
three sandwiches			
one banana			
seven bananas			
one bar of chocolate			
five bars of chocolate			
a big pack of crisps			
a glass of orange juice			

Shopping

5 Look at the shopping lists. What do you know already?

A
- milk
- fish
- 4 apples
- ice-cream
- crisps

B
- cheese
- 3 tomatoes
- salad
- cornflakes
- orange juice

C
- cheese
- 6 bananas
- spaghetti
- cake
- 2 mangoes

D
- 7 carrots
- coffee
- bread
- chocolate
- soup

E
- ice-cream
- tea
- fish
- milk
- bread

6 Do you like the food on these lists?
Draw a happy face for the food you like.
Draw a sad face for the food you don't like.

7 Look at the supermarket in the Pupil's Book.
Can you find the food on the lists? What is missing?
With which shopping list can you find everything in the supermarket, with list A, B, C, D or E?

What I like

8 Write your own chant. Read the example first.

I like chocolate,

And I like milk,

I like apples,

And I like eggs,

But I don't like cheese!

I like ______________________

And I like ______________________

I ______________________

And ______________________

But I don't ______________________

My shopping list

9 Now you go on a school outing. What do you buy? Write your own shopping list.

____

____

____

____

____

____

____

____

____

____

10 Are the things on your list good for you? Look at your list. What makes you:

– run faster **1**

– feel good and healthy **2**

– feel tired and full **3**

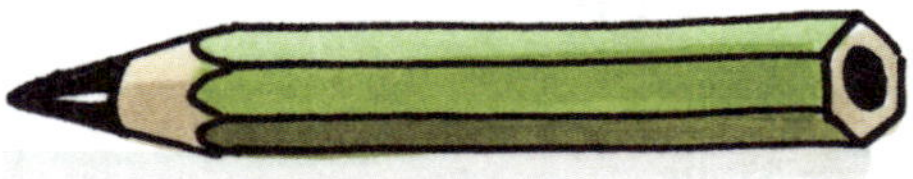

Make a milkshake

11 Listen carefully. Can you find everything? Then number the pictures.

Banana milkshake

1 banana

1 cup of milk

ice-cream

1. put 2 spoons of ice-cream in a jar
2. mash the banana with a fork
3. put the mashed banana into the jar with the ice-cream and stir
4. add the milk
5. put the lid on the jar
6. shake it all together
7. pour it into a glass

12 Draw a line from the pictures to the word in the recipe.

*13 Make a milkshake.
Look at the recipe and follow it carefully.*

Puzzle

14 What a mess!
Find the missing letters and fill them in.

1 san ___ wich

2 ___ ear

3 te ___

4 sa ___ ad

5 ___ ilk

6 ___ ppl ___

7 ___ omat ___

8 ___ ce-crea ___

9 ___ hocolat ___

10 ___ anan ___

15 Evaluation

I like page ___ in the Pupil's Book and page ___ in the Activity Book.

The funniest word: ___

I can say: ___

I remember these words: ___

This unit was: ___ great ☺ ___ ok 😐 ___ boring ☹ ___ hard

Through the year

Clothes

1 Listen and find the clothes on the line. Draw a circle around the clothes you hear.
2 Can you put the clothes into the baskets? Give each basket a number.

3 Look at Fabian and Tamsin. Fabian lives in Switzerland. Tamsin lives in Australia.

January in Switzerland

It is

This is Fabian in January

January in Australia

It is

This is Tamsin in January

Fabian's clothes are:

Tamsin's clothes are:

Weather

4 Write one of these words into each picture:
sun, rain, snow, rainbow, wind, clouds.

+

=

5 Write three words from this list under each picture.

rainy cloudy windy hot cold cool wet dry sunny warm snowy

6 Fill in the missing words.

sun **rainbow** **wind**

warm **cold** **wet** **dry** **rainy**

windy **April** **August**

jump **sit down** **kick**

It's spring. It isn't December, it's a__________. The s__________ is shining, and it is r__________ at the same time! So, there is a beautiful r__________. We're wearing jackets because it's not w__________. The path is all w__________ because of the rain. So we j__________ from one puddle to the next. That's fun!

7 What's the weather like?

It's ____________
in Geneva.

____ ____________
at the South Pole.

____ ____________
in Cairo.

____ ____________
in ____________

____ ____________
____ ____________

What's the weather like in
____________ *?*
____ ____________
____ ____________

8 Can you find these places on the world map?

9 Find the odd one out. Then write a new line and give it to a friend.

	hot		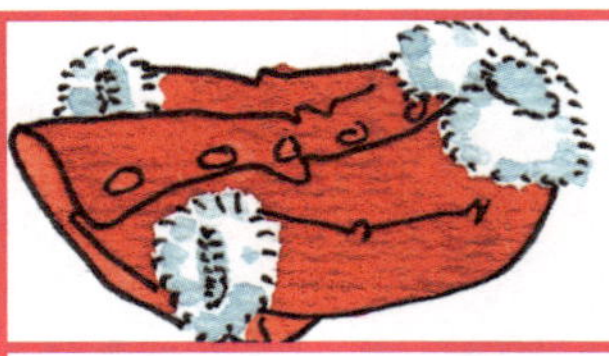
wet			
windy		cold	
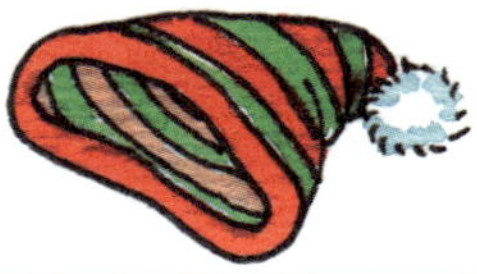		cloudy	snowy

10 Listen to the weather forecast.
What's the weather like in the morning?
In the afternoon?
In the evening?

11 Get dressed! Write a list of the clothes you can wear in this weather and then ask two friends what they wear.

In the morning I can wear

In the afternoon I can wear

In the evening I can wear

The weather around the world

12 Find the weather in a newspaper or ask somebody who knows.

Vancouver New York Perth Johannesburg New Delhi London Berne

date ______	weather	good clothes
 ______		
 ______		
 ______		
 ______		
 ______		
 ______		
 ______		

13 Evaluation

I like page ______ in the Pupil's Book and page ______ in the Activity Book.

The funniest word: ______. I can say: ______

I remember these words: ______

This unit was: ☐ great ☺ ☐ ok 😐 ☐ boring ☹ ☐ hard 💣

Around the clock

1 Look at the Pupil's Book. What time is it?

In Perth it's **4 pm**. What time is it in New York? ______

In London it's **8 am**. What time is it in New Delhi? ______

In New York it's **3 am**. What time is it in Johannesburg? ______

2 Ask a partner more questions like this.

3 What are they doing? Look at the Pupil's Book and listen to the CD.

In Vancouver it's midnight. David is ______ in bed.

In New York it's three o'clock at ______. Julie, her mother, her brother and the cat are ______.

In London it's already ______. It's eight o'clock and Mike is at home. He is eating ______.

In Johannesburg it's ten o'clock in the morning. Afzal is at ______. He is standing in front of the ______ and singing a song.

In New Delhi it's one o'clock in the ______. Shanoo is eating ______ in the cafeteria.

In Perth it's 4 o'clock in the afternoon. Sue is ______ outside with her ______.

Use the words in this box:

morning, dog, night, lunch, breakfast, playing, blackboard, sleeping, sleeping, school, afternoon.

4 And Marco? What is he doing?

______

______

5 Draw the time. Look at page 26 in the Pupil's Book to help you.

It's five to six

It's a quarter to three

It's twenty-five past eleven

It's half past one

7:10 or ten past seven

or

or

or

or

or

6 Before and after 12 o'clock noon.

IN GERMAN	IN ENGLISH
6:00 Uhr	6 am
9:00 Uhr	________________
11:00 Uhr	________________
12:00 Uhr	12 noon

IN GERMAN	IN ENGLISH
13:00 Uhr	1 pm
17:00 Uhr	________________
18:00 Uhr	________________
22:00 Uhr	________________

The mistake

7 Complete the clocks and write the sentences.

I'm running out the door. Time to get up. I'm brushing my teeth.
Oh no! It's Sunday! I'm getting dressed. I'm putting on my shoes.
I'm having breakfast. I'm running to school. I'm packing my school bag.

8 Choose the correct information for each child.

	gets up		school starts		school is out	
	5:30	6:30	8:15	8:45	3:00	3:15
	7:13	7:30	8:15	9:00	2:55	3:05
	6:45	7:15	7:30	8:30	3:00	3:45
	7:00	8:00	8:40	9:00	3:50	3:15
	8:00	8:25	8:30	9:00	1:00	4:00
	6:45	7:15	8:45	9:15	2:00	3:00

9 How do they go to school? Write the correct name under each picture.

10 Add it up!

1 How many days are in one week?

2 How many hours are in one week?

3 How many weeks are in one month?

4 How many weeks are in one year?

5 How many months are in one decade?

6 How many decades are in one century?

7 How many months do you go to school in one year?

11 Look at the chart. It shows Shanoo's week. This is a bar chart.

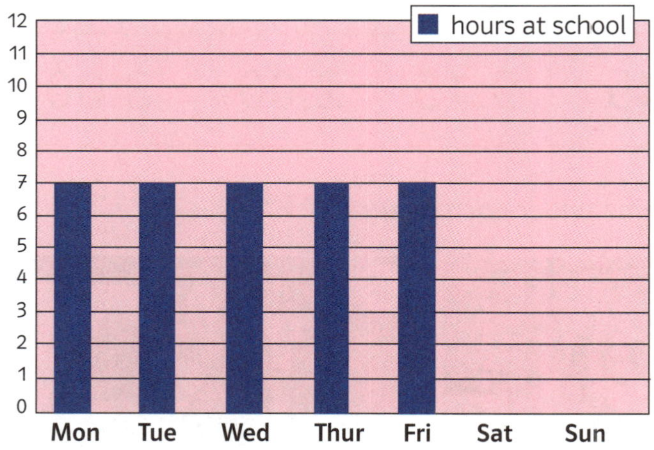

Shanoo is at school for hours every day.

Shanoo is not at school on

12 How many hours do you go to school on Monday, Tuesday, Wednesday, Thursday and Friday? Put them on a chart.

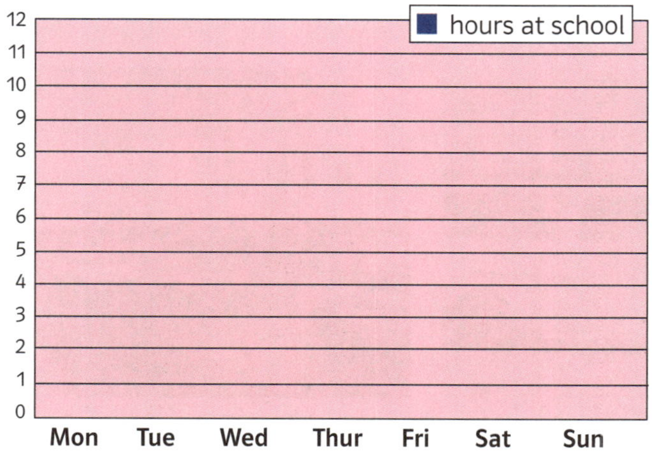

I am at school for hours on Monday.

I am at school for

I am

I am not at school on

13 Chart your day!

This is a pie chart.
24 hours

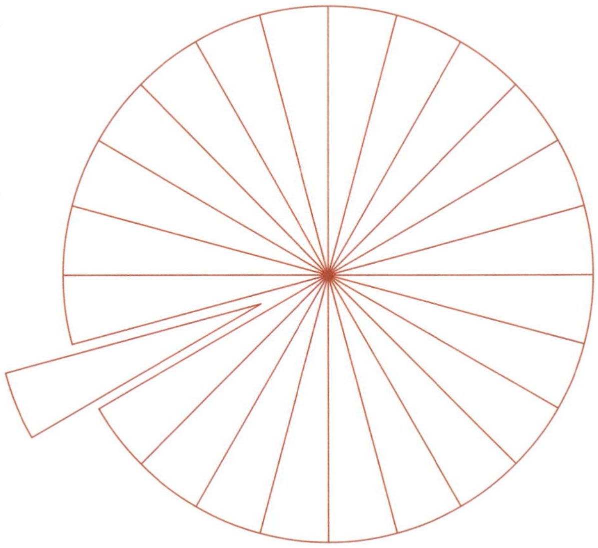

1 hour

Colour in the hours.

blue = hours of sleep
red = school hours
orange = homework
green = time to eat
yellow = time to play

What do you do the rest of the time?

14 Word search. Find eight words from this unit.
Then make your own word search with words from this unit and give it to a friend.

w	b	k	f	m	g	n	l	p	s
s	a	e	h	o	a	r	d	a	y
f	w	t	y	n	c	x	n	r	t
n	l	u	c	t	l	h	z	m	l
w	c	n	g	h	o	u	r	a	y
p	g	i	b	n	c	m	i	o	t
t	n	m	t	w	k	d	k	l	m
z	p	v	x	g	n	z	w	p	t
k	z	r	c	u	t	m	p	t	h
h	s	t	s	e	c	o	n	d	m

15 Evaluation

I like page ____ in the Pupil's Book and page ____ in the Activity Book.

The funniest word: ____. I can say: ____

I remember these words: ____

This unit was: ☐ great ☺ ☐ ok 😐 ☐ boring ☹ ☐ hard 💣

Unit 6

The house

1 Draw the rooms in your house. Complete the words.

k _ tch _ n

b _ thr _ _ m

l _ v _ ng r _ _ m

b _ dr _ _ m

______

______

2 Describe your house.

My house has ______ rooms. It has one living room and one kitchen.

It also has ___ bedrooms, ___ bathroom(s), ______

3 Colour the furniture to match the words.

bed desk bookcase

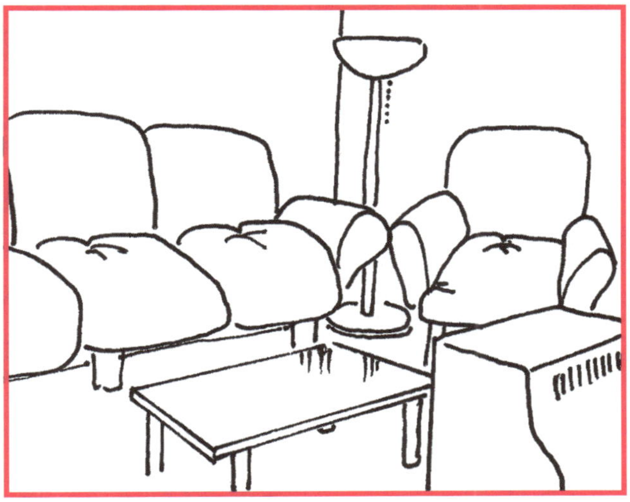

armchair sofa lamp television

shower bathtub toilet

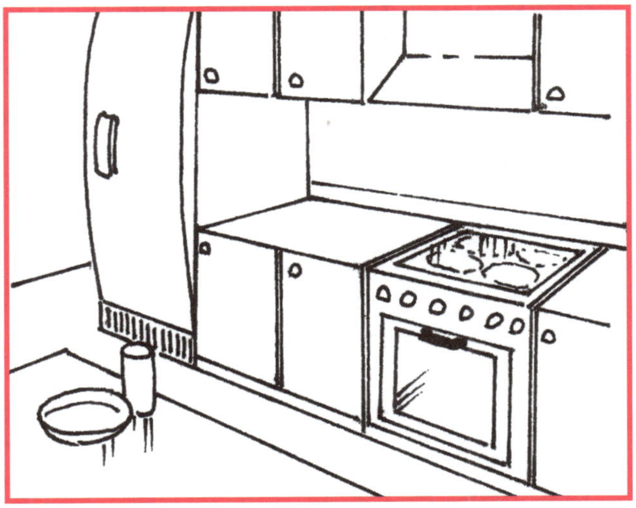

cooker fridge cupboard table

4 Complete the words.

arm		vision
cup		chair
tele		board

bath		robe
ward		case
book		tub

5 Where is the apple? Draw the apple in the picture.

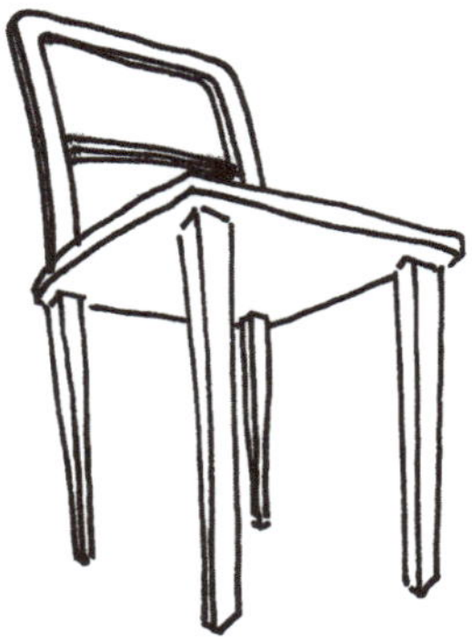

The apple is under the chair.

The apple is in the fridge between the milk and the yogurt.

The apple is on the table.

The apple is next to the lamp.

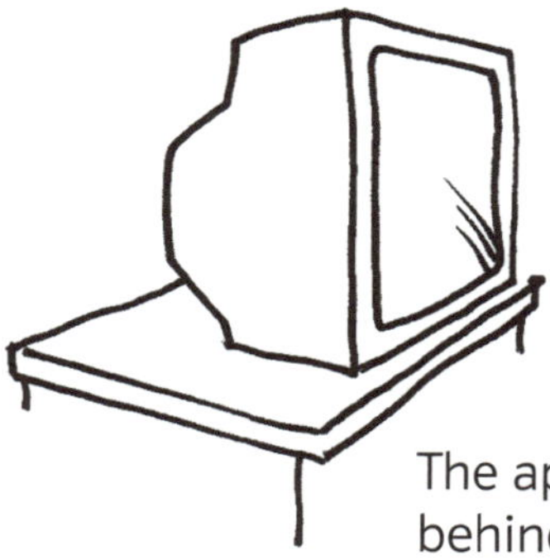

The apple is behind the television.

I am sitting at the table eating an apple.

6 Listen and number the pictures.

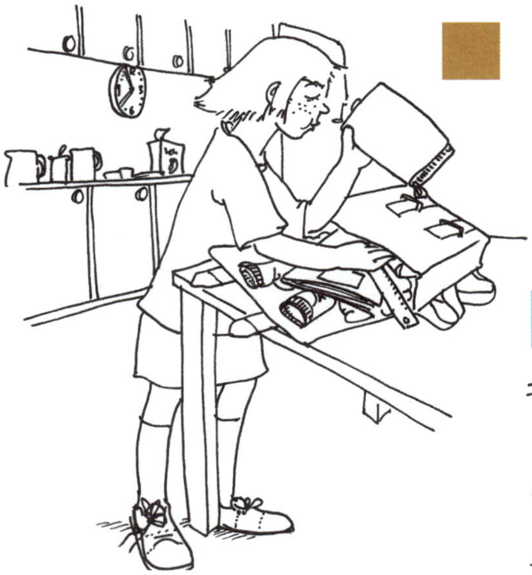

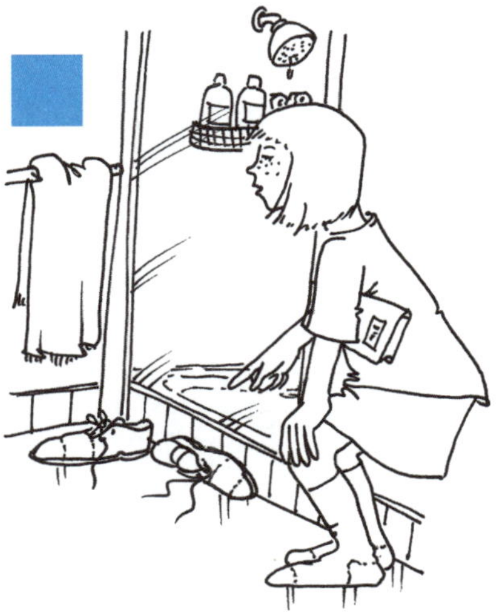

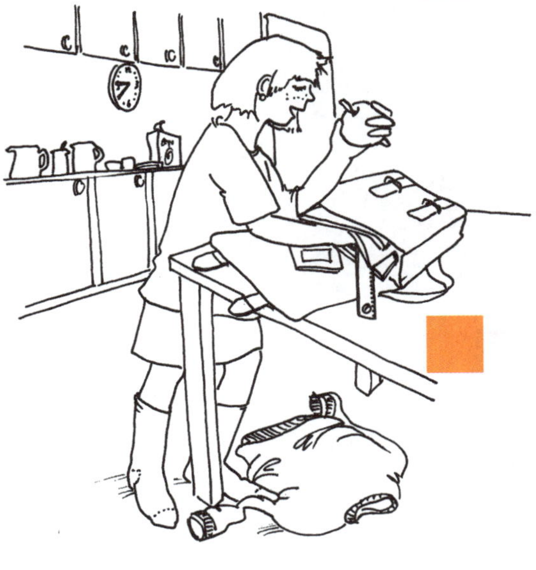

7 Tell the story.

Sally can't find her pencil case. It's not ______ the schoolbag.

She looks ______ the table.

She looks ______ the books.

She looks ______ the sofa.

She looks ______ the shower.

She looks ______ the wardrobe.

She looks ______ the bed.

She looks ______ the desk.

between in on under behind in next to under

8 Find the hidden objects in the picture.

9 Hide something in the classroom. Your partner must ask questions to find it.

10 Make a sentence with the words.

	log cabin		glass.
	tent		wood.
	farm house		bricks.
A	skyscraper	is made of	mud.
	castle		stones.
	tepee		straw.
	mud house		cloth.
An	igloo		ice.

Example: *A tepee is made of cloth.*

11 A good house. Draw a house to fit the picture.
Why do you think it is a good house for this place?

12 Read the poem.

There was an old woman who lived in a shoe.
She had so many children, she didn't know what to do.
She gave them some soup without any bread,
Then kissed them all sweetly and sent them to bed.

13 Can you write a poem? Your teacher can help with the words.

There was a ______ who lived in a ______.
He/she had so many ______, he/she didn't know what to do.
He/she gave them ______ without ______,
Then ______ them all ______
and sent them ______.

14 Evaluation

I like page ______ in the Pupil's Book and page ______ in the Activity Book.

The funniest word: ______. I can say: ______

I remember these words: ______

This unit was: ☐ great ☺ ☐ ok 😐 ☐ boring ☹ ☐ hard 💣

Let's show what we know

1 Find the right answers to the questions.

1 What does the family in Unit 3 want to pull out?

☐ carrot	☐ turnip	☐ tomato	☐ potato

2 The three little pigs and the big bad …

☐ fox	☐ tiger	☐ bear	☐ wolf

3 Sue from Unit 1 lives in …

☐ Switzerland	☐ Canada	☐ Australia	☐ the United States

4 The heart … blood through our body.

☐ pumps	☐ jumps	☐ runs	☐ puts

5 How fast is a storm?

☐ 120 km/h	☐ 60 km/h	☐ 90 km/h	☐ 30 km/h

6 How many years are in a decade?

☐ twelve	☐ five	☐ twenty	☐ ten

7 Your aunt is …

☐ your mother's sister	☐ your father's daughter	☐ your brother's sister	☐ your uncle's mother

8 The Eiffel Tower is in …

☐ London	☐ Paris	☐ New York	☐ Geneva

9 If you mix blue and yellow you get …

☐ pink	☐ green	☐ brown	☐ orange

10 The toe bones are connected to the …

☐ leg bones	☐ foot bones	☐ head bone	☐ hip bone

11 Which clock wakes you in the morning?

☐ the grandfather clock	☐ the cuckoo clock	☐ the alarm clock	☐ the sundial

12 Look at the big picture of the house in your Pupil's Book (p. 30–31). Where is the dog?

☐ in the attic behind the chair	☐ in the kitchen under the chair	☐ in the hall under the stairs	☐ in the kitchen under the table

2 Complete the sentences.

1 The skeleton is made of ________

2 When it's autumn in Switzerland, it's ________ in Australia.

3 Half past one is 1:30. A quarter to four is ________

4 A castle is made of ________

5 In Canada people speak French and ________

6 An ________ a day keeps the doctor away.

7 What comes after Sunday? ________

8 What do you wear on your head? ________

9 The sun is high in the sky. It's not winter, it's ________

10 It's made of ice-cream and banana. What is it? ________

3 Now find questions of your own. Use the Pupil's Book and Activity Book to help you.

____

____

____

____

4 Ask two friends your questions and try to answer their questions.

5 Can you do the crossword and find the hidden word?

DOWN
1 a house made of mud
2 a part of your leg
3 body part under your head
4 sweet bread
5 you can drink out of it
6 60 minutes
7 a very high house
8 you can write with it
9 you can write on it with chalk
10 your bed is in this room
11 you sit at it

ACROSS
12 counts the sunny hours only (plural)
13 head, … knees and toes
14 a yellow fruit
15 an orange vegetable
16 summer, … winter
17 clothing for your hands
18 a light wind
19 a log cabin is made of this
20 there's a fridge and a cooker in this room

Quiz
Can you find the hidden word?

Happy Birthday

Ordinal numbers

1 Find the correct group for each ordinal number.

1 2 3 4 5 6 7 8 9 10 11 12 13 20 21 22 23 30 31 32 33 40 41 42 43 50 51 52 53

th

st

nd

rd

When is your birthday?
2 Listen to the children and find out when their birthday is. Draw a line to the correct date.

Sue  1st August

Afzal  3rd October

Julie  12th April

Shanoo  18th May

David  9th November

Mike 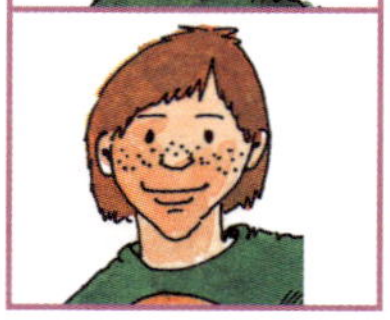 22nd January

3 When is your birthday? Write the day, month and year.

4 Now ask three friends and write the dates down.
When is your birthday?

Name	Day	Month	Year

My birthday party

5 You want to have a birthday party. What do you need? Write down the food you want to buy and the games you want to play.

Things to eat:

Things to drink:

Games to play:

Now compare your list with the list of a friend. Have you or your friend forgotten anything?

Christmas

Rudolph the red-nosed reindeer

You know Dasher and Dancer and Prancer and Vixen,
Comet and Cupid and Donner and Blitzen,
But do you recall the most famous reindeer of all?

Rudolph the red nosed reindeer
had a very shiny nose,
And if you ever saw it,
you would even say it glows.

All of the other reindeer
used to laugh and call him names,
They never let poor Rudolph
join in any reindeer games.

Then one foggy Christmas eve,
Santa came to say:
"Rudolph, with your nose so bright,
won't you guide my sleigh tonight?"

Then how the reindeer loved him
as they shouted out with glee:
"Rudolph, the red-nosed reindeer,
you'll go down in history!"

We wish you a Merry Christmas

We wish you a Merry Christmas,
We wish you a Merry Christmas,
We wish you a Merry Christmas and a Happy New Year!

Let's all do a little clapping,
Let's all do a little clapping,
Let's all do a little clapping and spread Christmas cheer.

We wish you a Merry Christmas …

Let's all do a little jumping
Let's all do a little jumping
Let's all do a little jumping and spread Christmas cheer.

We wish you a Merry Christmas …

Let's all do a little …

1 Add your own verses.

ENGLISCH-PORTFOLIO

TEIL 1

Das bin ich

Name:

Geburtstag:

Geburtsland:

Foto einkleben

Meine erste Englischlektion

Datum:

- Monday
- Tuesday
- Wednesday
- Thursday
- Friday
- Saturday
- Sunday

Meine Sprachen

Diese Sprachen kann ich sprechen:

Mein Lieblingswort:

Diese Sprachen habe ich auch schon gehört:

Diese Sprachen möchte ich lernen:

Meine Englischwörter

ENGLISCH-PORTFOLIO

TEIL 2

Datum:

Ich habe schon folgende Themen gehabt:

Ich kann auf Englisch verstehen,	*Kann ich schon ☺*	*Muss ich noch üben 😐*
wenn ich etwas aus meiner Schultasche nehmen soll.		
wenn ich mein Kursbuch öffnen soll.		
wenn ich jemandem etwas geben soll.		
wenn ich etwas für meine Lehrerin / meinen Lehrer machen soll.		
wenn mich jemand nach dem Namen fragt.		
wenn mich jemand begrüsst.		
wenn sich jemand vorstellt.		
wenn mir jemand seine Familie vorstellt.		

Ich verstehe:

- ❑ einzelne Wörter im Hörtext.
- ❑ einzelne Wörter, wenn die Lehrerin /der Lehrer spricht.
- ❑ kurze Hörtexte im Kursbuch.
- ❑ die Lehrerin/den Lehrer.

Ich kann lesen.

- ❑ Ich kann Wörter aus dem Kursbuch lesen und verstehen.
- ❑ Ich kann ganze Sätze aus dem Kursbuch lesen und verstehen.
- ❑ Ich kann eine kurze Geschichte aus dem Kursbuch lesen und verstehen.

Ich kann sprechen.

- ❑ Ich kann bis 20 zählen.
- ❑ Ich kann meine Familie vorstellen.
- ❑ Ich kenne die Namen von Ländern auf Englisch.
- ❑ Ich kann Teile meines Körpers und meines Gesichts benennen.
- ❑ Ich kann Turnübungen beschreiben.

MY ENGLISH WORDS

colours

body

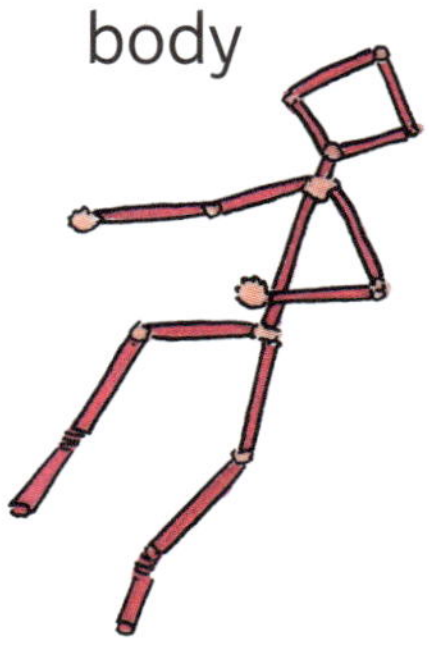

I can say: ______________________________

____

____

____

My favourite song, chant, rhyme or poem: 

____

ENGLISCH-PORTFOLIO

TEIL 3

Datum:

Ich habe schon folgende Themen auf Englisch gehabt:

Ich verstehe	*Ja, das kann ich schon gut.*	*Ich bin noch am lernen.*	*Das ist noch etwas schwierig für mich.*
das, was die Lehrerin/der Lehrer auf Englisch sagt.			
die Aufgaben im Buch.			
die Hörtexte, ohne dass ich jedes Wort kenne.			
die englischen Bezeichnungen für die verschiedenen Nahrungsmittel.			
die englischen Bezeichnungen für die verschiedenen Kleidungsstücke.			
die englischen Bezeichnungen für die verschiedenen Jahreszeiten.			
die englischen Bezeichnungen für die verschiedenen Wetterphänomene.			
die Spielregeln für das Leiterlispiel auf Englisch.			
die Geschichte *We're going to find a cave.*			

Ich kann auf Englisch sagen,	*Ja, das kann ich schon gut.*	*Ich bin noch am lernen.*	*Das ist noch etwas schwierig für mich.*
was ich gerne esse.			
was ich nicht so gerne esse.			
was ich in einem Lebensmittelgeschäft kaufen kann.			
welche Nahrungsmittel gesund sind.			
welche Nahrungsmittel nicht so gut sind für mich.			
welches Wetter wir im Moment haben.			
was ich zum Beispiel im Winter am besten anziehe.			

Das kann ich lesen und verstehen:	*Ja, das kann ich schon gut.*	*Ich bin noch am lernen.*	*Das ist noch etwas schwierig für mich.*
die Aufgabenstellungen im Pupil's Book und im Activity Book			
ein Rezept für Milkshakes			
eine kurze Geschichte			

MY ENGLISH WORDS

food

clothes

weather

I can say: ____________________

____

____

____

My favourite song, chant, rhyme or poem: 

____

ENGLISCH-PORTFOLIO

TEIL 4

Datum:

Ich habe schon folgende Themen auf Englisch gehabt:

Das kann ich schon auf Englisch!

Ich verstehe:

❍ einfache ❍ einige ❍ fast alle Anweisungen meiner Lehrerin/meines Lehrers.
❍ einfache ❍ einige ❍ fast alle Anweisungen auf der Kassette.
❍ einfache ❍ einige ❍ fast alle Teile einer kurzen Geschichte, wenn meine Lehrerin/mein Lehrer sie erzählt.
❍ einfache ❍ einige ❍ fast alle Teile einer kurzen Geschichte auf der Kassette.
❍ einfache ❍ einige ❍ fast alle Fragen an mich, auch wenn sie manchmal wiederholt werden müssen.

Ich kann lesen und verstehen:

❍ einfache ❍ einige ❍ fast alle Wörter, die wir im Buch geübt haben.
❍ einfache ❍ einige ❍ fast alle kurzen Sätze, die wir im Buch geübt haben.
Reime, Chants und Lieder, die wir im Buch gelernt haben: ❍ ein bisschen ❍ teils ❍ gut
Geschichten, die wir im Buch gelernt haben: ❍ ein bisschen ❍ teils ❍ gut

Sprechen:

❍ einfache ❍ einige ❍ viele Sätze, die wir geübt haben, kann ich sagen.
❍ einfache ❍ einige ❍ viele neue Sätze kann ich aus Wörtern, die wir gelernt haben, bilden.
❍ einfache ❍ einige ❍ viele Reime, Chants und Lieder, die wir geübt haben, kann ich aufsagen.
❍ einfache ❍ einige ❍ fast alle Teile einer kurzen Geschichte, die wir geübt haben, kann ich erzählen.
❍ einfache ❍ einige ❍ viele einfache Fragen zu Themen aus dem Buch kann ich beantworten.

Ich verstehe,	*Kann ich schon.* ☺	*Muss ich noch üben.* 😐
wenn jemand mich nach der Zeit fragt.		
wenn jemand mir die Zeit sagt.		
wenn jemand sein Haus beschreibt.		
wenn jemand sein Zimmer beschreibt.		

MY ENGLISH WORDS

house

time

My favourite song, chant, rhyme or poem: 

Sentences I can use: